The Music in Me

Paulette Jackson

The Music In Me
Copyright © 2016 Paulette Jackson

ISBN: 978-1-938950-65-0

Graphic Designer: Rob King
Interior Layout: Tony Bradford

Greater is He Publishing
9824 E. Washington St,
Chagrin Falls Ohio 44023
P O. Box 46115
Bedford Ohio, 44146

"When I wake up and go to sleep at night thinking about music, I know in my soul it's what I should be doing."

To my daughters, Paris and Brooke
My love is and always will be here for you . . .

Bambi
Thank you for loving and believing in me . . . unconditionally

Mother, Dad, and my brother Michael
Thank you for the gifts of song & dance. These gifts will live on in
me and my children . . . Miss You All

Contents

"Music can take you places far away, you can be anyone you want through music."

Preface

I've always wanted to write about what my passions were in my life for a long time but never really thought about in book form until I was talking to a friend of mine who also wrote a book about his life's journey (Thanks, Spanky). Even right after his book came out, I still wasn't thinking of writing one of my own. Just writing out how I felt about my life and my love for music, for the Arts as a whole.

Only after having another conversation with William (Spanky to those who knew him through high school) did it dawn on me to write a book!

When I wake up in the mornings, working my "day job" and before I go to sleep, I have music in my head and my heart.

I'm either listening to (like right now) music, watching a TV special centered on the Arts or reading about music and artists.

"Music Isn't What I Do, It's Who I Am" . . . Always.

I hope this book gives you a little insight into me, my soul. When you have a passion inside you, never let it die . . .

"Music seems to always say the things you've been wanting to say but couldn't."

CHAPTER 1
Since I Could Remember

I think I was around four or five, not much older than that, when I remembered listening to the radio, or to one of my mother's aunt's records or radio playing. It wasn't one type of music, it was Jazz, Motown, Pop and Classical, but I used to try and sing along to those songs I really liked.

Seems the more I sang, the better I seemed to become at doing it. My mother would listen to me most times and smile.

I've always had a love for music, certain melodies (which I didn't know what that really meant at that age LOL). I guess, no, I know it's how I felt when I heard a certain song and/or singer.

So, the older I became, the more I came to really appreciate it and then really wanted to understand what I was singing. So, in my early teenage years, I began to record songs off the radio and then would play them back, verse by verse, and write down the lyrics so I could know what I was singing instead of what I thought it said. (Smile)

Let's go back a minute. I also remember, before my teenage years, listening a lot to AM radio stations because at that time, it seemed all the good stations were on AM frequency. My favorite was WJMO 1490 because they played a lot of R&B, Motown! I so miss those days . . .

Sometimes, it was hard to go to sleep because my mother would often still have the radio playing, and I could hear it in my room. I didn't mind though, I just wanted to hear it.

Most times, it helped me fall asleep. Not that the music in any way was boring or dull; it was soothing and warm to me. Then, I found myself, as I got older, having my radio on at night, thinking I would miss my favorite song if I turned it off. Still makes me feel that way . . .

You may have similar memories of music you love from your own childhood. Now might be a good time to reflect on those memories and share the music in you!

_____

_____

_____

_____

_____

_____

_____

_____

_____

_____

_____

CHAPTER 2
In the Blood

M y parents were artists, or at least they wanted to be, I believe. My mother was a graceful dancer and my father had a beautiful tenor singing voice. I believe my mother could have gone further in her dance career than she did.

My parents, as I was told, met at the Karamu House here in Cleveland, a very historic community theater/ arts center. Some of today's African-American actors came from Karamu House!

Both my parents tried to make a go of their respective artistic crafts but didn't quite get there, regrettably. My father, though, felt he needed to make "real" money, so he made the decision to quit singing as a profession but kept singing out of sheer love for it.

My brother, Michael, was an excellent musician and

composer.

I know my love and passion for the Arts came from my parents; it's in the blood, and I'm very proud of that.

So, of course later on, when I got older, I started writing and wanted my father and brother Michael to look at my work and tell me what they thought of my lyrics. I remember getting up in the middle of the night, most nights, when a melody hit me, and I would start writing based off those melodies.

Eventually, Michael wanted to put a few of my songs to music; how excited was I! By the way, my brother wrote for the legendary O'Jays, was a member of Kinsman Dazz (later to become The Dazz Band) and Jean Carne, just to name a few.

Okay, back to my influences. Just having the opportunity to work with my brother, words cannot express. I learned a lot from him about the business side of the music industry. Also, he took me around some very influential artist like the O'Jays, Jean Carne and Gerald Levert.

Not to mention some other excellent musicians he played with and were friends with. I keep in contact with them to this day.

I also remember going out on the road or to shows my brother performed at with a reggae band, Harambe.

As I'm writing about my parents' and brother's influences, I get teary-eyed because they are all in heaven now . . . together.

My love for music, dance and the arts as a whole lives on in me because of them. Thank you and much love to you all . . .

What is the fuel behind your passion? Take a moment to discuss your own passion in life. Talk about the people who have breathed life into your passion. How have they inspired you to do what you love?

_____

_____

_____

_____

_____

_____

_____

_____

_____

_____

_____

"Music is not only what I strive to do, it's who I am inside."

CHAPTER 3
High School

I was attending junior high school and really didn't like it because kids would pick with me sometimes, and I felt out of place, not popular. Even then, I knew I wanted to sing or be in fashion but knew no one at my junior high school understood me. Maybe they thought I was stuck up or something because of the dreams I had. I don't know.

Then, something happened that would change my life! A childhood friend (Michael Medcalf) had left the school I was attending and was telling me about his new school. He knew how much I loved to sing and dance and started telling me about the Cleveland School of the Arts.

CSA was on the ast side of Cleveland (we were both living on the west side at that time). He told me how to contact them about auditioning for the next school year.

So, of course I ran home to tell my mother. She made a couple of calls, and next thing I knew I received info in the mail about how/where to audition!!

I let my father know because the school was near where he lived, so he met me at the school the morning I auditioned, a Saturday.

I auditioned for dance because I thought I had a better chance of getting in, even though my real love was singing. I was so very nervous about the thought of auditioning.

Well, it worked because about a week or two later, I came home from school, and my mother told me she had received the letter saying I made it!! I would attend the Cleveland School of the Arts as a ninth grader, 1983-1984 school year! Thank you, Michael.....

Finally, a place where I could express my love for the arts. My mother did ask, however, why I didn't audition for vocal music? She always felt I had a beautiful voice. (Smile)

Anyway, eventually I did switch my major from dance to vocal music, but not without having to sing for, now one of my favorite music teachers, Dr. William Woods (he was just Mr. Woods then), who became

"Papa Woods" to most of his students.

I'm so glad I made the transition to vocal music. I feel it was a better choice even though I still liked dance.

I got to be a part of theater productions, off-campus field trips and performances. I even had the opportunity to travel to the Pittsburgh School of the Arts. They had nothing on CSA though. (Smile)

We all have exciting events in our lives and things we are proud of. What are some of the most memorable things that have happend in your life? Talk about some accomplishments that you feel good about.

_____

_____

_____

_____

_____

_____

_____

_____

_____

_____

_____

"I am proud to say that music is in my blood & soul and I wouldn't have it any other way."

CHAPTER 4
CSA Friends/Family

The thing I really loved about being at CSA was the people, from students to faculty. Cleveland School of the Arts became my second home, and the students, upper and lower classman, became my extended family. To this day, at the age of almost forty-eight, I'm still very close friends with my fellow CSA alums and wouldn't trade any of them for anything in the world.

Let's back track a little. I spent four wonderful years at the Cleveland School of the Arts and met who would become my husband and father of my children there.

My sophomore year, I got the opportunity to audition for Top 20 Vocal Ensemble, a group I wanted to be a part of my freshman year but wasn't quite ready for. Well, I made it. I became a member of the Vocal Ensemble, and I felt accomplished and proud.

I was already a member of the choir but wanted to become a member of that group. I guess I had something to prove to myself, that I was good enough.

As graduation approached, two years later, I was feeling sad because I really didn't want to leave. I loved it there.

I felt so blessed and proud to be a student at the first performing arts high school in Cleveland (many compared our school to the TV show "Fame").

I thank God for that amazing opportunity and surrounding me with extraordinary people. CSA will live in me forever . . .

Perhaps there is a special place that will always live inside of you. Think about that place. Now, take some time to share everything about the place that makes it special to you.

CHAPTER 5
The Music & Dance Lives On

A fter I graduated, I later that year got married to my CSA high school sweetheart, and a couple of years later, we had our first daughter, Paris. Then a year after that, Brooke was born; they're beautiful.

As my daughters got older, I noticed they were developing a love for music, especially Paris at the time. I remember one evening while I was in another room, their dad called me into the living room where Paris was. Just a baby then, she was in her little roller right in front of the TV and Whitney Houston was singing, "You're All the Man I Need." My baby was singing along with her with arms stretched wide as though she was on stage!

I really did shed a tear watching her. She reminded me a lot of myself. I remember telling my dad and everyone else about it; my dad chuckled and smiled.

Brooke has developed a love for dance; my mother would be proud. She's a praise dancer for church and performs various programs, or at least she did for a while. I watched her so intensely one evening at a program she was dancing for, I shed a tear for her too, I was so proud.

They are both adults now and still have a love for music and dance, even though they may not admit it to me. Although different styles, still, the love is there, I believe. Brooke even wanted to open an arts center for kids. I believe she will someday soon.

I don't push my daughters into going into the arts professionally, but I won't discourage them either. I want them to follow their own passions in life and be happy and never have any regrets about their choices.

So, Mother, Dad and Michael, your gifts live on in us . . .

Are there any gifts or or talents that have been passed down in your own family? Talk about some of those gifts you hope to pass on to your own children, grandchildren, nieces, nephews, or even younger siblings.

CHAPTER 6
Later Life

As life progressed, I divorced, worked, lived, loved, dreamed and have been through many trials and tribulations. I didn't have the greatest of childhoods, but music was and is my refuge.

I have been working all types of "jobs" and never was truly happy at any of them because I felt I should've been doing music and/or fashion, another love of mine, or something in the arts because that's where my heart has always been and always will be.

I've always felt I'm a free spirit, an artist, and until I get an opportunity to do what I really love full-time, I will never be fulfilled, ever.

I know I have to at least try. Do some of you reading this right now feel the same way?

I'm forty-seven, and I still live, breathe, and dream the arts, music. So, now the kids are grown, I'm not married anymore and feel like I may not be able to live the dreams I had thirty years ago, but I still can at least go for some of them, and writing this book is a start to that, I feel.

I wanted to write about my love and passion for not only music, but for the arts as a whole. It's been in me since I was little and has not left me to this day, which can only mean, as I've said earlier, it's in the blood, baby!!

All of us have put certain things on hold due to circumstances. We can lose our stride in the general flow of everyday life. What are some of the dreams you have put on hold or have all but forgotten? What's holding you back now?

CHAPTER 7
Today's Music

Anyone that truly knows me knows that I love 'Ol school music, The O'Jays, The Stylistics, The Spinners, The Temptations etc.... I could go on and on. Today's music gives me hives for the most part! I don't like a lot of it. There's no creativity, just a lot of sampling, and real instruments are hardly used anymore, ugh!

I appreciate REAL musicianship and artistry, I love it. I'm so very disappointed with today's artists, if you want to call most of them that. Don't get me wrong now. Not all of today's artists suck (excuse the expression). There are some very talented, gifted musicians and singers out here today who, in my opinion, are very underrated.

But I believe that's what happens to real artists, the ones that don't give in and go with the status quo and really do what feels good and right for them.

Unfortunately, a lot of artists don't get the credit and exposure they so deserve.

I say don't give in to the hype and keep writing, singing real music, stay true to your gifts and it will pay off in the long run.

Artists today should really do some heavy research and learn all they can about the business side of music as well as taking music theory courses. Find out about musicians/singers that have paved the way for us all to do what we love to do. The sacrifices they've had to make to get to where they wanted to be professionally and artistically.

The music today, for the most part, lacks meaning and passion. My personal thank you to the artists that are keeping REAL music alive.

You may share these feelings about the music of today. How would you compare today's artists to those of the past, the 60s & 70s, the 80s, or even the 90s? Are there any artists today that you can appriciate? Who are they, and why do you feel they should be recognized?

_____

_____

_____

_____

_____

_____

_____

_____

_____

_____

CHAPTER 8
A Little Inspiration

I have been through a lot in my life, no more or no less than anyone else, and I'm not unique in that area. However, knowing the things I've been through, even today, and different people I've encountered, good and bad, I'm still standing for a reason, God!

I didn't always believe in Him, but I'm so glad I do now! No, I'm not real religious, but I definitely believe in God's grace in my life. Now, at forty-seven years old, soon to be forty-eight, God willing, I finally feel like this is my season to shine. I'm doing voice-over work, writing again (this book for one), poems, and songs included!

I'm also getting back to my first love of music, and I don't even have to be up front. I'm perfectly happy working and recording in a studio; just the opportunity to sing again, professionally, would be an extreme gift within itself.

I've said this before to others and will tell all reading this book right now, please don't give up on your dreams and passions. More importantly, don't let anyone ever tell you what you can't do. It doesn't matter what your background is, who your parents are, or where you live. You can do whatever you put your mind to. Go for it!

Yes, it will be hard; yes, it will be scary; yes, you will get rejection and you may have to distance yourself from people that are not being positive and supportive. Let no one hold you back, including yourself, which I've done too many times.

Pull your strength and confidence from a higher being and surround yourselves with like-minded people. Learn new things every day to help you get to the next phase of your journey.

YOU CAN DO IT!

Surely, you have seen some difficult times in your life, but if you're reading this, that means God's has pulled you through. This alone should give you the courage to after what you love. Talk about some of the tests and trials the grace of God has brought you through in your life.

_____

_____

_____

_____

_____

_____

_____

_____

_____

_____

"The melodic tones and the way a singer delivers a song, sometimes make me cry, not because I'm sad, but because of the beauty of it."

CHAPTER 9
Influences

There have been many influences in my life, good and bad. For the bad influences, especially those who were negative and non-supportive of what I really wanted to do, I say thank you because it made me push harder, especially at this stage of my life, to work even harder to achieve my passions and set new goals for myself. Also, to take past dreams and re-direct them to new ones, still in the Arts, just some new avenues.

So again, thank you to all the naysayers!

To the positive, "tough love" influences, which included my mother, father and brother Michael, thank you for believing in me and my gifts. I may not have listened then, just out of sheer laziness and fear, but your words did sink in throughout the years, especially when I really started to realize I did not want to work for other people's dreams for the rest of my life.

I have to believe in God and myself to get this done, and part of that is surrounding myself with individuals in positions that can help me achieve my goals and let the Lord take the lead.

My musical influences are too many to list, but here are a few – My father, brother (Michael), Nancy Wilson, Billie Holiday, Donny Hathaway, Rachelle Ferrell, Frank McComb and Anita Baker. Their voices and styles of singing touch me in a way that is indescribable.

I find myself in tears at times, listening to them and the delivery and passion in which they tell their lyrical stories. It takes a gifted vocalist to be able to touch a person in that way.

Be your biggest positive influence and the rest will follow. Bottom line, which took me a while to get, if you don't believe in you, no one else will either.

Maybe you also see negativity as a way to push harder, or maybe you are blessed enough to have positive people in your corner cheering you on. Where do you turn to for encouragement? If you turn to the bible, what passages or stories do you find particularly inspiring?

_____

_____

_____

_____

_____

_____

_____

_____

_____

_____

CHAPTER 10
The Music in Me

Music will always be in my soul because, as I've said earlier in this text, it's in my blood, and I'm so very proud of that. I pray the music, love for the Arts, will live on in my children and grandchildren.

Even though my parents and brother, Michael, are no longer with me, what each has taught and instilled in me will stay with me until I leave this earth. That's one of the things I know that no one will ever take away from me. I believe it is God-given so, for that reason alone, no one can touch it.

I love everything about music, the Arts, especially how it can (and I believe will) continue to bring people together from all walks of life. God, how amazing is that! With all of our differences, music is the one thing that truly brings us together.

Not only music, but the Arts as a whole. I'm so

very excited about the rest of my artistic life, my life period, happy about the directions I'm going in and the people whom I've met recently and those who've been with me since the beginning, reconnecting. They've shared, listened and given constructive criticism when necessary, but all the while being supportive and open.

No matter what, I know "the music" will always be in me. May it be in you as well . . .

"Music is love
Music is life
It can make you cry,
it can make you laugh

Music is..............
forever!"

www.ingramcontent.com/pod-product-compliance
Lightning Source LLC
Chambersburg PA
CBHW071646040426
42452CB00009B/1776